OVERCOMING SOCIAL ANXIETY

A Journey of Self Discovery and Empowerment

From the best selling author of **"Depression: The Path to Healing"**

DAN OHTEE

DEDICATION

"Dedicated to all those who have ever felt held back by the shackles of social anxiety, may this book be a beacon of hope and a guiding light on your journey towards self-discovery, empowerment, and freedom. May you find the courage to face your fears, the strength to overcome them, and the resilience to rise above them. May you discover a life of confidence, connection, and purpose, and may you never let

social anxiety hold you
back again."

"To anyone who has ever
felt anxious in a crowd,
may this book help you find
your voice and your place
in the world."

"To all those who are ready
to break free from social
anxiety and unlock their
full potential, this book is
for you."

<u>TABLE OF CONTENTS</u>

INTRODUCTION

Understanding Social Anxiety

Social anxiety is a complex and multifaceted mental health condition characterized by an excessive and persistent fear of social situations. This condition affects a significant portion of the population, causing substantial distress, impairment, and limitation in daily life. It is essential to understand the underlying causes, symptoms, and impact of social anxiety to develop effective strategies for management and recovery.

Causes and Risk Factors: A Multifaceted Approach

Social anxiety is caused by a combination of genetic, environmental, and psychological factors, including:

- Genetic predisposition: Individuals with a family history of social anxiety may be more prone to developing the condition.
- Imbalances in brain chemistry: Neurotransmitters such as

serotonin and dopamine play a crucial role in regulating mood and anxiety.

- Traumatic events or negative social experiences: Past experiences can shape an individual's perception of social situations.

- Personality traits: Perfectionism, low self-esteem, and negative self-talk can contribute to social anxiety.

Symptoms: Physical, Emotional, and Behavioral Manifestations

Social anxiety can manifest in various ways, including:

- Physical symptoms: Rapid heartbeat, sweating, trembling, or blushing in social situations.
- Emotional symptoms: Feelings of fear, anxiety, or panic when interacting with others.
- Behavioral symptoms: Avoidance of social situations, difficulty making friends, or impaired daily functioning.

Impact: Far-Reaching Consequences

Social anxiety can have a significant impact on daily life, affecting:

- Relationships: Difficulty forming and maintaining relationships due to fear of rejection or judgment.
- Work or school performance: Impaired academic or professional success due to avoidance of social situations.
- Participation in social activities, hobbies, or interests: Limited engagement in activities due to fear or anxiety.

By understanding the complexities of social anxiety, individuals can take the first step towards recovery and developing effective coping strategies.

Part 1:
Understanding
Social Anxiety

Chapter 1: The Mask of Social Anxiety: Uncovering the Hidden Struggle

Social anxiety is a pervasive mental health condition that affects numerous individuals worldwide, causing them to conceal their genuine emotions and thoughts behind a facade of confidence and composure. This mask serves as a coping mechanism, enabling individuals to navigate social situations without revealing their true feelings of fear, anxiety, and self-doubt.

As Sarah, a 28-year-old marketing professional, recounts, "I've always felt like I'm wearing a mask in social situations. I'm terrified of being judged or rejected, so I put on a smile and pretend to be someone I'm not. But it's exhausting, and I feel like I'm losing myself in the process."

The mask of social anxiety is a carefully crafted persona, designed to conceal the individual's true emotions and thoughts. It is a coping mechanism that enables individuals to avoid rejection, judgment, and ridicule from others. However, this mask also perpetuates feelings of shame, guilt, and inadequacy, as individuals struggle to reconcile their authentic selves with the persona they present to the world.

"I feel like I'm living a lie," says John, a 35-year-old teacher. "I'm afraid to speak up in meetings or share my ideas with my colleagues. I'm terrified of being seen as stupid or incompetent. So I just nod and smile, and hope no one notices my silence."

The reasons behind the mask of social anxiety are multifaceted and complex. They include:

- Fear of rejection and judgment: The fear of being rejected or judged by others is a powerful motivator for individuals with social anxiety.
- Fear of being seen as weak or vulnerable: Individuals with social anxiety may also fear being seen as weak or vulnerable,

and so they put on a mask to hide their true feelings.
- Fear of losing control or being overwhelmed: Social situations can be overwhelming for individuals with social anxiety, and so they hide behind a mask to avoid feeling overwhelmed.

"I avoid social situations at all costs," says Emily, a 22-year-old student. "I'm afraid of being overwhelmed by my emotions, and I don't know how to cope. So I just stay home, alone, and try to avoid the anxiety."

The impact of the mask of social anxiety on daily life is profound. It can affect:

- Relationships: Superficial connections and difficulty forming deep, meaningful relationships.
- Work or school performance: Impaired academic or professional success due to avoidance of social situations.
- Mental health: Increased stress, anxiety, and depression.
- Physical health: Poor sleep, digestive issues, and

compromised immune function.

Breaking free from the mask of social anxiety requires seeking help and support. This can involve:

- Cognitive-behavioral therapy (CBT)
- Exposure therapy
- Mindfulness and relaxation techniques
- Support groups
- Self-help strategies

As Sarah notes, "Seeking help was the best decision I ever made. I learned to confront my fears and anxieties, and to accept myself for who I am. I'm still working on it, but I feel like I'm finally living my authentic life."

By understanding the complexities of the mask of social anxiety and seeking help and support, individuals can begin to break free from the constraints of this debilitating condition. It's time to unveil the concealed struggle and shatter the mask of social anxiety, embracing a life of authenticity, connection, and purpose.

Chapter 2: The Roots of Social Anxiety: Exploring the Causes

Social anxiety, a pervasive mental health condition, affects millions worldwide, causing individuals to feel excessively self-conscious, fearful, and anxious in social situations. But what are the roots of this debilitating condition? What causes individuals to feel like they are living in a constant state of fear and apprehension?

We will explore the complex causes of social anxiety, delving into the psychological, environmental, and biological factors that contribute to its development. We will also examine real-life experiences and popular quotes to gain a deeper understanding of this condition.

Psychological Factors

Social anxiety often stems from negative thought patterns, low self-esteem, and past experiences. As the celebrated author, Brené Brown, notes, "Shame is the fear of being unlovable, unworthy, and unaccepted." When individuals experience shame or embarrassment, they may develop social anxiety as a coping mechanism.

Environmental Factors

Environmental factors, such as upbringing, culture, and social media, also play a significant role in the development of social anxiety. As the psychologist, Dr. Jean

Twenge, notes, "Social media has created a culture of competition, where individuals feel like they need to present a perfect image."

Biological Factors

Biological factors, including genetics, brain chemistry, and neurobiology, also contribute to social anxiety. As the neuroscientist, Dr. Daniel Siegel, notes, "The brain is wired to respond to threats, and social anxiety can be a result of an overactive threat response."

Sarah, a 28-year-old marketing professional, recounts her experience with social anxiety: "I've always felt like I'm on edge in social situations. I'm afraid of being judged or rejected. But after seeking help, I realized that my social anxiety was rooted in my childhood experiences and negative thought patterns."

John, a 35-year-old teacher, shares his experience: "I used to avoid social situations altogether. But after therapy, I learned to confront my fears and rewire my brain. Now, I feel more confident and self-assured."

Social anxiety is a complex condition with multiple causes. By understanding the psychological, environmental, and biological factors that contribute to its development, individuals can begin to break free from the constraints of this debilitating condition. As the poet, Maya Angelou, notes, "You may not control all the events that happen to you, but you can decide not to be reduced by them."

By seeking help, confronting fears, and rewiring negative thought patterns, individuals can overcome social anxiety and live a more authentic, confident life.

In conclusion, social anxiety is a multifaceted condition with deep roots in psychological, environmental, and biological factors. By understanding these causes, individuals can begin to address and overcome their social anxiety.

As the psychologist, Dr. Marsha Linehan, notes, "The goal of therapy is not to eliminate emotions, but to learn to tolerate them."

By learning to tolerate and manage emotions, individuals can develop the skills and confidence to navigate social situations with ease.

In addition, seeking support from mental health

professionals, support groups, and loved ones can provide individuals with the tools and resources needed to overcome social anxiety.

As the famous quote goes, "You are not alone, and you are not a burden."

By recognizing that social anxiety is a common and treatable condition, individuals can begin to break free from the constraints of this debilitating condition and live a more authentic, confident life.

In the words of the poet, Rupi Kaur, "You do not have to be defined by your anxiety. You are more than your fears."

By embracing this message and seeking help, individuals can overcome social anxiety and live a life that is true to who they are.

Chapter 3: The Impact of Social Anxiety: How It Affects Daily Life

Social anxiety is a mental health condition that affects millions of people worldwide, causing significant distress and impairment in daily life. It can lead to feelings of fear, anxiety, and self-doubt, making everyday social interactions a daunting task.

Social anxiety can affect relationships, causing individuals to feel isolated and disconnected from others. It can also impact work or school performance, leading to missed opportunities and unfulfilled potential. Furthermore, social anxiety can have a profound impact on overall well-being, causing individuals to feel stressed, anxious, and depressed.

Real-life experiences show that social anxiety can be debilitating, causing individuals to avoid social situations, sabotage relationships, and feel like they are living in a constant state of fear.

However, there is hope for healing and recovery. By understanding the impact of social anxiety and seeking help, individuals can begin to break free from its constraints.

Popular quotes remind us that we are not alone, and that there is strength in vulnerability. As Nelson Mandela said, "The greatest glory in living lies not in never falling, but in rising every time we fall." By seeking help and support, individuals can overcome social anxiety and live a life that is true to who they are.

Social anxiety has a profound impact on daily life, affecting relationships, work or school performance, and overall well-being. However, with the right support and resources, individuals can overcome social anxiety and live a fulfilling life.

Seeking Help and Support

Seeking help and support is the first step towards overcoming social anxiety. This can include talking to a mental health professional, joining a support group, or practicing self-help strategies such as mindfulness and relaxation techniques.

Building Self-Esteem

Building self-esteem is also an important part of overcoming social anxiety. This can involve identifying and challenging negative self-thoughts, practicing self-compassion, and developing a growth mindset.

Developing Coping Mechanisms

Developing coping mechanisms is also crucial for managing social anxiety. This can include learning relaxation techniques, practicing deep breathing, and engaging in physical activity.

In conclusion, social anxiety is a common mental health condition that can have a significant impact on daily life. However, with the right support and resources, individuals can overcome social anxiety and live a fulfilling life. By seeking help and support, building self-esteem, and developing coping mechanisms, individuals can learn to manage their social anxiety and improve their overall well-being.

Remember, overcoming social anxiety takes time and effort, but it is possible. With the right mindset and support, individuals can learn to navigate social situations with confidence and ease.

Chapter 4: The Many Faces of Social Anxiety: Types and Symptoms

Social Anxiety is a complex condition with multiple faces, manifesting in different types and symptoms. "Fear is not something to be ashamed of. It's a natural part of life. But when it becomes debilitating, it's time to take action."

We will explore the various types and symptoms of social anxiety, delving into the ways it affects individuals and society.

Types of Social Anxiety

1. Generalized Social Anxiety Disorder: Characterized by excessive and persistent fear of social situations, leading to avoidance and significant distress.

2. Specific Social Phobia: Involves fear of a specific situation, such as public speaking or meeting new people.

3. Performance Anxiety: Concerns fear of being judged or evaluated, often in work or academic settings.

Symptoms of Social Anxiety

1. Excessive self-consciousness and fear of being judged

2. Difficulty making friends or maintaining relationships

3. Avoidance of social situations or events

4. Physical symptoms such as rapid heartbeat, sweating, and trembling

5. Negative self-talk and self-criticism

- "The greatest glory in living lies not in never falling, but in rising every time we fall." - Nelson Mandela

Social anxiety is a multifaceted condition with various types and symptoms, affecting individuals and society in profound ways. By understanding and acknowledging its many faces, we can work towards creating a more supportive and inclusive environment. Remember, social anxiety is not a sign of weakness, but rather a sign of strength in seeking help and support. As the poet, Rupi Kaur, notes, "You do not have to be defined by your anxiety. You are more than your fears."

The Importance of Seeking Help and Support

Seeking help and support is crucial for individuals struggling with social anxiety. This can include talking to a mental health professional, joining a support group, or practicing self-help strategies such as mindfulness and relaxation techniques. With the right support and resources, individuals can learn to manage their social anxiety and improve their overall well-being.

Building a Support Network

Building a support network of family, friends, and mental health professionals is essential for individuals struggling with social anxiety. Having a supportive network can provide individuals with a sense of security and comfort, allowing them to feel more confident in social situations.

Practicing Self-Care

Practicing self-care is also essential for individuals struggling with social anxiety. This can include engaging in activities that bring joy and relaxation, such as exercise, hobbies, or spending time in nature. By prioritizing self-care, individuals can improve their overall mental health and well-being.

In conclusion, social anxiety is a complex condition that affects individuals in different ways. By understanding its various types and symptoms, seeking help and support, building a support network, and practicing self-care, individuals can learn to manage their social anxiety and improve their overall well-being. Remember, social anxiety is not a sign of weakness, but rather a sign of strength in seeking help and support.

Part 2: Breaking Free from Social Anxiety

Chapter 5: The Power of Self-Awareness: Identifying Negative Thought Patterns

Self-awareness is the ability to have an honest and accurate understanding of your thoughts, feelings, and behaviors. It is the foundation of personal growth and development, allowing individuals to identify areas for improvement and make positive changes. As the renowned psychologist, Carl Jung, noted, "Your vision will become clear only when you look into your heart. Who looks outside, dreams; who looks inside, awakens."

One of the most significant benefits of self-awareness is the ability to identify negative thought patterns. These patterns can hold individuals back from reaching their full potential, causing unnecessary stress and anxiety. By becoming aware of these patterns, individuals can begin to challenge and change them, leading to a more fulfilling and meaningful life.

Negative thought patterns can manifest in various ways, including:

- Self-doubt: "I'm not good enough."
- Catastrophizing: "This is a disaster."
- All-or-nothing thinking: "I'm a total failure."

These patterns can be deeply ingrained, making it difficult to recognize and challenge them. However, with self-awareness, individuals can begin to notice when these patterns arise and take steps to reframe them in a more positive and realistic light.

As the celebrated author, Maya Angelou, said, "Do the best you can until you know better. Then, when you know better, do better." Self-awareness allows individuals to know better, to understand their thoughts and behaviors, and to make positive changes.

By identifying negative thought patterns, individuals can:

- Develop a more realistic and positive mindset
- Improve their mental health and well-being
- Enhance their relationships with others
- Increase their self-confidence and self-esteem

Self-awareness is a powerful tool for personal growth and development. By identifying negative thought patterns, individuals can begin to challenge and change them, leading to a more fulfilling and meaningful life. Remember, self-awareness is the first step towards positive change. As the poet, Rupi Kaur, noted, "You do not have to be defined by your thoughts. You are more than your mind."

The Benefits of Self-Awareness

Self-awareness has numerous benefits, including:

- Improved emotional regulation: By being aware of your thoughts and emotions, you can better manage your emotions and

respond to situations more effectively.
- Increased self-acceptance: Self-awareness allows you to understand and accept yourself, including your strengths and weaknesses.
- Enhanced relationships: By being aware of your own emotions and needs, you can communicate more effectively and build stronger relationships with others.
- Increased self-confidence: Self-awareness can help you develop a more positive self-image

and increase your self-confidence.

- Improved decision-making: By being aware of your own biases and thought patterns, you can make more informed decisions.

As the famous psychologist, Daniel Goleman, noted, "Self-awareness is the ability to monitor our inner world - our thoughts, feelings, and bodily sensations - as we move through our day."

Practicing Self-Awareness

Practicing self-awareness takes time and effort, but it is worth it. Here are some tips to help you increase your self-awareness:

- Practice mindfulness: Pay attention to your thoughts, emotions, and bodily sensations in the present moment.
- Keep a journal: Writing down your thoughts and feelings can help you identify patterns and gain insights.
- Seek feedback: Ask for feedback from trusted friends, family, or colleagues.

- Practice self-reflection: Take time to reflect on your thoughts, feelings, and behaviors.

In conclusion, self-awareness is a powerful tool for personal growth and development. By identifying negative thought patterns and practicing self-awareness, individuals can lead more fulfilling and meaningful lives. Remember, self-awareness is the first step towards positive change. As the poet, Rumi, noted, "The wound is the place

where the light enters
you."

Chapter 6: Challenging Negative Self-Talk: Reframing Thoughts and Beliefs

Negative self-talk is a pervasive and debilitating phenomenon that affects countless individuals worldwide. It is the constant stream of critical and demeaning inner dialogue that can erode self-confidence, undermine self-worth, and hinder personal growth. As Dr. Kristin Neff, a renowned psychologist, notes, "Self-compassion is not self-pity, but rather treating yourself with kindness, concern, and support." This journey of challenging negative self-talk requires a willingness to confront and reframe deeply ingrained thoughts and beliefs.

Recognizing Distorted Thinking Patterns

The first step in challenging negative self-talk is to recognize the distorted or unhelpful thinking patterns that perpetuate it. These patterns can include all-or-nothing thinking, catastrophizing, and self-doubt. By becoming aware of these patterns, individuals can begin to challenge and reframe them in a more balanced and constructive light. As Maya Angelou, the celebrated author, said, "Do the best you can until you know better. Then, when you know better, do better."

Cognitive-Behavioral Therapy (CBT)

One effective strategy for challenging negative self-talk is cognitive-behavioral therapy (CBT). CBT helps individuals identify and challenge negative thought patterns, reframe distorted beliefs, and develop more adaptive coping skills. As Dr. David Burns, a psychologist, notes, "The way we think about ourselves and our experiences can either empower or debilitate us." Through CBT, individuals can learn to reframe their thoughts in a more positive and supportive way.

Mindfulness-Based Interventions

Another approach is mindfulness-based interventions, which cultivate present-moment awareness and non-judgmental acceptance. Mindfulness practices, such as meditation and deep breathing, can help individuals develop a more compassionate and accepting relationship with themselves. As Thich Nhat Hanh, a Buddhist teacher, said, "To love oneself is to love all." By cultivating mindfulness, individuals can learn to observe their thoughts without judgment and develop a greater sense of self-awareness.

Self-Compassion Practices

In addition, self-compassion practices, such as self-kindness, self-forgiveness, and self-appreciation, can help individuals develop a more positive and supportive inner dialogue. As Dr. Kristin Neff notes, "Self-compassion is not selfish, but rather essential for our well-being and happiness." By practicing self-compassion, individuals can learn to treat themselves with kindness and understanding, rather than criticism and judgment.

Embracing Self-Compassion

Self-compassion is a powerful tool for challenging negative self-talk. By treating ourselves with kindness, understanding, and acceptance, we can begin to shift our inner dialogue and develop a more positive and supportive relationship with ourselves. As Dr. Kristin Neff notes, "Self-compassion is not a feeling, but a practice." It involves cultivating mindfulness, recognizing our common humanity, and practicing self-kindness.

Practicing Self-Kindness

Self-kindness involves treating ourselves with the same kindness and compassion that we would offer to a friend. It involves being gentle, understanding, and supportive, rather than critical and judgmental. As Maya Angelou said, "You alone are enough. You have nothing to prove to anyone." By practicing self-kindness, we can begin to quiet the critical voice and cultivate a more positive and supportive inner dialogue.

Recognizing Our Common Humanity

Recognizing our common humanity involves acknowledging that we are all imperfect, vulnerable, and connected. It involves recognizing that we all struggle with negative self-talk and that it is a common human experience. As Thich Nhat Hanh said, "We are all in the same boat." By recognizing our common humanity, we can begin to cultivate a sense of connection and understanding, rather than isolation and shame.

Mindfulness and Self-Awareness

Mindfulness and self-awareness are essential for challenging negative self-talk. By cultivating present-moment awareness, we can begin to observe our thoughts without judgment and develop a greater sense of self-awareness. As Dr. Daniel Siegel notes, "Mindfulness is the practice of being present in the moment, without judgment." By cultivating mindfulness and self-awareness, we can begin to recognize the distorted thinking patterns that perpetuate negative self-talk and challenge them in a more constructive way.

Challenging negative self-talk requires a commitment

to reframing thoughts and beliefs, cultivating self-awareness, and practicing self-compassion. By recognizing the distorted thinking patterns that perpetuate negative self-talk and replacing them with more balanced and constructive ones, individuals can develop a more positive and supportive inner dialogue. Remember, as the poet Rumi noted, "You are not a drop in the ocean. You are the entire ocean in a drop."

Chapter 7: Building Self-Esteem: Cultivating Confidence and Self-Worth

Self-esteem is the foundation of a healthy and fulfilling life. It is the sense of self-worth, confidence, and value that enables individuals to navigate life's challenges with resilience and positivity. As the renowned psychologist, Dr. Nathaniel Branden, notes, "Self-esteem is the reputation we acquire with ourselves."

Cultivating Confidence

Confidence is a critical component of self-esteem. It involves believing in oneself, one's abilities, and one's worth. As the celebrated author, Maya Angelou, said, "You alone are enough. You have nothing to prove to anyone." Confidence can be cultivated through achievements, positive affirmations, and supportive relationships.

Recognizing Self-Worth

Recognizing self-worth involves acknowledging one's value, strengths, and accomplishments. As the poet, Rumi, noted, "You are not a drop in the ocean. You are the entire ocean in a drop." Self-worth can be fostered through self-reflection, self-care, and self-compassion.

Embracing Imperfections

Embracing imperfections is essential for building self-esteem. It involves accepting oneself, flaws and all, and recognizing that imperfections are a natural part of being human. As the actress, Emma Stone, said, "I think everybody has their own struggles, and I think everybody has their own imperfections."

Practicing Self-Care

Practicing self-care is vital for building self-esteem. It involves nurturing oneself, physically, emotionally, and mentally. As the wellness expert, Audre Lorde, noted, "Self-care is not selfish. It is a necessary act of self-love."

Developing a Growth Mindset

Developing a growth mindset is essential for building self-esteem. It involves embracing challenges, persisting through obstacles, and viewing failures as opportunities for growth. As the psychologist, Dr. Carol Dweck, notes, "The growth mindset is based on the belief that abilities can be developed."

Practicing Positive Self-Talk

Practicing positive self-talk is vital for building self-esteem. It involves using affirmations, reframing negative thoughts, and cultivating a supportive inner dialogue. As the motivational speaker, Tony Robbins, said, "The way we talk to ourselves matters."

Embracing Authenticity

Embracing authenticity is critical for building self-esteem. It involves being true to oneself, embracing individuality, and rejecting societal expectations. As the poet, Oscar Wilde, noted, "To be yourself in a world that is constantly trying to make you something else is the greatest accomplishment."

Building Resilience

Building resilience is essential for maintaining self-esteem. It involves developing coping skills, learning from failures, and persisting through adversity. As the psychologist, Dr. Angela Duckworth, notes, "Grit is about working on something you care about so much that you're willing to stay with it even when it gets difficult."

Conclusion

Building self-esteem requires a commitment to cultivating confidence, recognizing self-worth, embracing imperfections, practicing self-care, developing a growth mindset, practicing positive self-talk, embracing authenticity, and building resilience. By fostering a positive and supportive relationship with oneself, individuals can develop a strong sense of self-esteem, enabling them to navigate life's challenges with resilience and positivity.

Maya Angelou: "You are the sum total of everything you've ever seen, heard, eaten, smelled, been told, forgot – it's all there. Everything influences each of us."

"Do the best you can until you know better, then when you know better, do better"

Chapter 8: Exposure Therapy: Gradual Steps to Overcoming Fear

"Courage is not the absence of fear, but rather the judgment that something else is more important than fear." – Ambrose Redmoon

Exposure therapy is a highly effective treatment approach for overcoming fear and anxiety. It involves gradually and systematically exposing individuals to the feared object, situation, or activity, while using relaxation techniques to manage anxiety. This essay will explore the gradual steps involved in exposure therapy and how it can help individuals overcome fear.

Step 1: Identifying and Assessing Fears

"The first step to overcoming fear is to acknowledge and accept it." – Unknown

The first step in exposure therapy is to identify and

assess the fear. This involves understanding the nature of the fear, its severity, and how it affects daily life. A mental health professional can help individuals identify and assess their fears.

Step 2: Creating a Hierarchy

"Gradual exposure to the feared situation is the most effective way to overcome fear." – Dr. Edna Foa

Once the fear is identified and assessed, a hierarchy is created. This involves ranking the feared situations or objects from least to most anxiety-provoking. This hierarchy serves as a guide for the exposure process.

Step 3: Starting with Small Steps

"Small steps today, a better tomorrow." - Unknown

Exposure therapy begins with small steps.

Individuals start with the least anxiety-provoking situation or object on their hierarchy and gradually work their way up. This helps build confidence and reduces anxiety.

Step 4: Using Relaxation Techniques

"Relaxation is the key to reducing anxiety." - Dr. Herbert Benson

Relaxation techniques, such as deep breathing, progressive muscle relaxation, and visualization, are used to manage anxiety during exposure. These techniques help individuals calm their nervous system and reduce physiological responses.

Step 5: Processing and Reflecting

"Processing and reflecting on the exposure experience is crucial for success." - Dr. Barbara Rothbaum

After each exposure session, individuals process

and reflect on their experience. This involves discussing their feelings, thoughts, and physical sensations with their therapist. This step helps individuals integrate their experiences and solidify new learning.

"Exposure therapy is not about confronting fear head-on, but about gradually and systematically building confidence and resilience."

Exposure therapy is a powerful tool for overcoming fear and anxiety. By gradually and systematically exposing individuals to the feared object, situation, or activity, exposure therapy helps build confidence, resilience, and coping skills. As Ambrose Redmoon notes, "Courage is not the absence of fear, but rather the judgment that something else is more important than fear." With exposure therapy, individuals can learn to prioritize their values and goals over their fears, leading to a more fulfilling life.

The Benefits of Exposure Therapy

"Exposure therapy is a powerful tool for overcoming fear and anxiety, and can lead to significant improvements in daily life." – Dr. David F. Tolin

Exposure therapy has numerous benefits, including:

1. Reduced anxiety and fear
2. Increased confidence and self-efficacy
3. Improved daily functioning
4. Enhanced cognitive reappraisal
5. Increased resilience

Real-Life Experience: Overcoming Social Anxiety

"Exposure therapy helped me overcome my social

anxiety and live a more fulfilling life." – Rachel, age 29

1. Imaginal exposure: vividly imagining social scenarios
2. In vivo exposure: gradually confronting social situations

Through exposure therapy, Rachel learned to manage her anxiety, build confidence, and develop coping skills.

"Exposure therapy is a journey, not a destination. It takes courage, commitment, and patience, but the rewards are immeasurable."

Exposure therapy is a highly effective treatment approach for overcoming fear and anxiety. By gradually and systematically exposing individuals to the feared object, situation, or activity, exposure therapy helps build confidence, resilience, and coping skills. Remember, exposure therapy is a journey, and with the right mindset and support, individuals can overcome their fears and live a more fulfilling life.

Part 3:
Empowerment Strategies

Chapter 9: Mindfulness and Relaxation Techniques: Finding Calm in the Storm

"Social anxiety is like a storm, but mindfulness and relaxation are the anchors that keep us grounded."

Social anxiety can be a debilitating experience, making everyday interactions feel like a daunting task. However, mindfulness and relaxation techniques offer a powerful solution to overcome social anxiety and find calm in the storm.

Understanding Social Anxiety

"Social anxiety is not just shyness, it's a fear of being judged, evaluated, and rejected." – Dr. Aziz Gazipura

Social anxiety is a common mental health condition characterized by feelings of excessive fear, nervousness, and self-consciousness in social situations. It can lead to avoidance behaviors, missed opportunities, and a decreased quality of life.

The Power of Mindfulness

"Mindfulness is the practice of being fully present and engaged in the current moment, while cultivating a non-judgmental awareness of one's thoughts, feelings, and bodily sensations." - Jon Kabat-Zinn

Mindfulness techniques, such as meditation and deep breathing, help individuals become more aware of their thoughts, feelings, and physical sensations in the present moment. This increased awareness allows individuals to better manage their anxiety and respond to social situations more skillfully.

Relaxation Techniques: Calming the Nerves

"Relaxation is not something that you do, it's a state of being." - Deepak Chopra

Relaxation techniques, such as progressive muscle relaxation and visualization, help calm the nervous system, reducing feelings of anxiety and stress. These techniques can be used in conjunction with mindfulness practices to enhance their effectiveness.

Finding Calm in the Storm of Social Anxiety

"Courage is not the absence of fear, but rather the judgment that something else is more important than fear." - Ambrose Redmoon

By incorporating mindfulness and relaxation techniques into our daily lives, we can find calm in the storm of social anxiety. These techniques help us develop a greater sense of self-awareness, self-acceptance, and self-compassion.

"I used to avoid social gatherings due to my social anxiety. But after practicing mindfulness and relaxation techniques, I can now navigate these situations with ease and confidence." - Rachel, age 29

Tips for Overcoming Social Anxiety

1. Start small: Begin with small, low-stakes social interactions, such as chatting with a cashier or saying hello to a neighbor.
2. Practice mindfulness and relaxation: Regularly practice mindfulness and relaxation techniques to reduce overall anxiety levels.
3. Challenge negative thoughts: Notice and challenge negative self-talk and catastrophic thinking patterns.
4. Seek support: Connect with others who understand social anxiety, either through support

groups or online communities.

5. Be patient: Overcoming social anxiety takes time and effort, so be gentle and compassionate with yourself.

"Mindfulness and relaxation are the keys to unlocking a more confident, calm, and connected you."

By embracing mindfulness and relaxation techniques, we can find calm in the storm of social anxiety and overcome the fears that hold us back.

The Benefits of Mindfulness and Relaxation

"Mindfulness and relaxation are not just techniques, they are a way of life."

By incorporating mindfulness and relaxation techniques into our daily lives, we can experience numerous benefits, including:

1. Reduced anxiety and stress
2. Improved emotional regulation

3. Enhanced self-awareness
and self-acceptance
4. Increased confidence and
self-esteem
5. Better sleep quality
6. Improved relationships
7. Increased resilience and
ability to cope with
challenges

"I was diagnosed with
social anxiety disorder and
was struggling to cope with
everyday situations. But
after practicing
mindfulness and relaxation
techniques, I can now
navigate these situations
with ease and confidence. I

feel more calm, centered, and connected to myself and others." – Emily, age 27

Tips for Maintaining Calm in the Storm

1. Make mindfulness and relaxation a regular part of your daily routine
2. Start small and gradually increase your practice
3. Find what works best for you and stick to it
4. Seek support from others who understand social anxiety

5. Be patient and compassionate with yourself

"Mindfulness and relaxation are the anchors that keep us grounded in the storm of social anxiety."By embracing these techniques, we can find calm, confidence, and connection."

Remember, social anxiety is not a defining characteristic, but rather an opportunity for growth and self-discovery. By incorporating mindfulness and relaxation techniques into our daily lives, we can overcome the fears that hold us back and live a more empowered, resilient life. Start your journey today and discover a more calm, confident, and connected you.

Chapter 10: Effective Communication: Assertiveness and Boundary-Setting

Assertiveness: Finding Your Voice

"Assertiveness is not about being aggressive, it's about being clear and direct."

Assertiveness involves expressing your needs, wants, and feelings in a clear and respectful manner. It requires confidence, self-awareness, and a willingness to take risks. When you communicate assertively, you:

- Set clear boundaries
- Express your needs and wants clearly
- Listen actively
- Avoid passive or aggressive behavior

Popular Quote: "The most courageous act is still to think for yourself. Aloud."
- Coco Chanel

Boundary-Setting: Protecting Your Time, Energy, and Emotions

"Boundaries are not meant to keep people out, but to keep yourself in."

Boundary-setting involves establishing clear limits on what you are and are not comfortable with. It requires self-awareness, communication skills, and a willingness to say "no" when necessary. When you set boundaries, you:

- Protect your time, energy, and emotions
- Prioritize your needs and wants
- Avoid burnout and resentment
- Build trust and respect with others

Popular Quote: "You can't pour from an empty cup. Take care of yourself first."

Overcoming Social Anxiety through Effective Communication

"Effective communication is not about being perfect, it's about being present." - Unknown

Effective communication involves being present, aware, and authentic in your interactions with others. It requires:

- Active listening
- Empathy and understanding
- Clarity and directness
- Non-judgmental feedback

"The art of communication is the language of leadership." – James Humes

"Effective communication is the key to unlocking strong relationships, personal growth, and professional success."

Assertiveness and boundary-setting are essential components of effective communication. By speaking up with confidence and setting clear boundaries, individuals can overcome social anxiety, build stronger relationships, and live a more authentic, fulfilling life. Remember, effective communication is a skill that can be developed with practice, patience, and persistence. Start communicating effectively today and unlock your full potential!

Tips for Overcoming Social Anxiety

1. Start small: Begin with small, low-stakes social interactions, such as chatting with a cashier or saying hello to a neighbor.

2. Practice assertiveness: Speak up clearly and respectfully, and prioritize your own needs and wants.

3. Set boundaries: Establish clear limits on what you are and are not comfortable with, and be willing to say "no" when necessary.

4. Seek support: Connect with others who understand social anxiety, either through support

groups or online communities.

5. Be patient: Overcoming social anxiety takes time and effort, so be gentle and compassionate with yourself.

Popular Quote: "You are not alone in your struggles, and you are stronger than you think."

Effective communication is the key to unlocking a more confident, authentic, and fulfilling life. By practicing assertiveness and boundary-setting, individuals can overcome social anxiety and build stronger relationships.

Remember, overcoming social anxiety is a journey, and it's okay to take it one step at a time. With patience, persistence, and practice, you can develop the skills and confidence to navigate social situations with ease. Start your journey today and discover a more empowered, resilient you!

Chapter 11: Building a Support Network: Surrounding Yourself with Positivity

"The best way to find yourself is to lose yourself in the service of others." – Mahatma Gandhi

Overcoming social anxiety requires a supportive network of people who encourage and uplift you. Surrounding yourself with positivity can help you build confidence, develop coping skills, and achieve personal growth.

The Power of Positive Relationships

"Surround yourself with people who make you hungry for life, touch your heart, and nourish your soul." – Unknown

Positive relationships are essential for building a support network. These relationships can help you:

- Develop a sense of belonging and connection
- Build self-esteem and confidence
- Learn coping skills and strategies

- Stay motivated and inspired

"The people you surround yourself with are the people you become."

Building a Support Network

"You can't get to the top alone. You need a team to help you achieve your goals."

Building a support network requires effort and dedication. Here are some steps to help you get started:

1. Identify positive relationships: Surround yourself with people who uplift and support you.
2. Join a community: Connect with others who share similar interests and goals.
3. Attend events: Participate in events and activities that help you meet new people.
4. Volunteer: Help others through volunteering, which can help you build connections and a sense of purpose.

Popular Quote: "Alone we can do so little; together we

can do so much." – Helen Keller

The Benefits of a Support Network

"A support network is like a safety net, it's there to catch you when you fall."

A support network can provide numerous benefits, including:

- Emotional support: A listening ear and a comforting presence.
- Practical help: Assistance with tasks and responsibilities.

- Guidance: Advice and mentorship from experienced individuals.
- Encouragement: Motivation and inspiration to achieve your goals.

"You are stronger than you seem, braver than you believe, and smarter than you think." - Christopher Robin

"Building a support network is essential for overcoming social anxiety. Surround yourself with positivity, and you'll be amazed at the progress you can make."

Remember, building a support network takes time and effort, but it's worth it. With a positive support network, you can overcome social anxiety and achieve your goals. Start building your network today!

Tips for Building a Support Network

1. Be open and honest: Share your struggles and fears with others.
2. Listen actively: Pay attention to others and show that you care.

3. Be supportive: Offer help and encouragement to those in need.

4. Be patient: Building a support network takes time and effort.

5. Be proactive: Take the initiative to reach out to others and build connections.

"The greatest gift you can give someone is your time, because when you give your time, you are giving a portion of your life."

"Building a support network is a powerful way to overcome social anxiety.

By surrounding yourself with positivity and supportive people, you can achieve your goals and live a more fulfilling life."

Remember, building a support network is an ongoing process that requires effort and dedication. But with persistence and patience, you can build a strong support network that will help you overcome social anxiety and achieve your dreams. Start building your network today!

Chapter 12: Self-Care and Stress Management: Nurturing Your Mind, Body, and Spirit

"You can't pour from an empty cup. Take care of yourself first."

Overcoming social anxiety requires a holistic approach that incorporates self-care and stress management techniques. By nurturing your mind, body, and spirit, you can build resilience, reduce anxiety, and improve your overall well-being.

The Importance of Self-Care

"Self-care is not selfish. It is a necessary act of self-love and self-respect." - Danielle LaPorte

Self-care involves intentionally taking care of your physical, emotional, and mental health. This includes:

- Engaging in activities that bring you joy and relaxation
- Practicing mindfulness and meditation

- Getting enough sleep and exercise
- Eating a healthy and balanced diet

"Love yourself first, and everything else falls into line." – Lucille Ball

Stress Management Techniques

"Stress is not something that happens to us, it's something that happens within us." – Unknown

Effective stress management techniques include:

- Deep breathing exercises
- Progressive muscle relaxation
- Journaling and expressive writing
- Seeking social support from friends, family, or a therapist

"You are not a victim of your circumstances. You are a product of your decisions."

Nurturing Your Mind

"The mind is everything; what you think, you become." - Buddha

Nurturing your mind involves:

- Practicing positive self-talk and affirmations
- Engaging in mentally stimulating activities
- Learning to reframe negative thoughts and perspectives
- Embracing lifelong learning and personal growth

"Believe you can and you're halfway there." - Theodore Roosevelt

Nurturing Your Body

"The body is a temple, take care of it."
Nurturing your body involves:

- Engaging in regular exercise and physical activity
- Eating a healthy and balanced diet
- Getting enough sleep and rest
- Practicing self-care and self-compassion

"Take care of your body. It's the only place you have to live." - Jim Rohn

Nurturing Your Spirit

"The spirit is the spark that ignites the flame of life." – Unknown

Nurturing your spirit involves:

- Engaging in activities that bring you joy and purpose
- Practicing mindfulness and meditation
- Connecting with nature and the world around you
- Embracing your values and beliefs

"You are never too old to set another goal or to dream a new dream." - C.S. Lewis

"Overcoming social anxiety requires a holistic approach that incorporates self-care and stress management techniques. By nurturing your mind, body, and spirit, you can build resilience, reduce anxiety, and improve your overall well-being."

Remember, taking care of yourself is not selfish, it's essential. By prioritizing your self-care and stress management, you can overcome social anxiety and live a more fulfilling life. Start nurturing your mind, body, and spirit today!

Tips for Prioritizing Self-Care

1. Start small: Begin with one or two self-care activities and gradually add more.
2. Listen to your body: Pay attention to your physical and emotional needs.

3. Be consistent: Make self-care a regular part of your routine.
4. Seek support: Connect with others who prioritize self-care.
5. Be patient: Self-care is a journey, not a destination.

Popular Saying: "The best way to take care of others is to take care of yourself first."

Self-care and stress management are essential for overcoming social anxiety. By nurturing your mind, body, and spirit, you can build resilience, reduce anxiety, and improve your overall well-being. Remember, taking care of yourself is not selfish, it's essential."

Remember, overcoming social anxiety takes time, effort, and patience. But with a commitment to self-care and stress management, you can achieve your goals and live a more fulfilling life. Start your self-care journey today!

Part 4: Overcoming Obstacles and Maintaining Progress

Chapter 13: Overcoming Setbacks and Relapses: Staying on Track

"Fall seven times, stand up eight." – Japanese proverb

Overcoming social anxiety is a journey, not a destination. Setbacks and relapses are an inevitable part of the process, but they don't define your progress. With the right mindset and strategies, you can overcome obstacles and stay on track.

Understanding Setbacks and Relapses

"A setback is not a failure, it's a stepping stone to success."

Setbacks and relapses are temporary detours from your progress. They can be triggered by various factors, such as:

- High-pressure situations
- Negative self-talk
- Lack of self-care
- Unforeseen circumstances

"Don't watch the clock; do what it does. Keep going."
- Sam Levenson

Strategies for Overcoming Setbacks

"When you get knocked down, get back up again. And again. And again."

To overcome setbacks and relapses, try:

- Practicing self-compassion and self-forgiveness
- Reframing negative thoughts and perspectives
- Seeking support from friends, family, or a therapist
- Focusing on progress, not perfection

- Developing a growth mindset

"I have not failed. I've just found 10,000 ways that won't work." - Thomas Edison

Staying on Track

"Stay committed to your goals, but flexible in your approach."

To stay on track, remember:

- Celebrate small victories and milestones

- Break down large goals into smaller, manageable steps
- Create a support network and accountability system
- Practice self-care and stress management techniques
- Stay positive and focused on your progress

"You don't have to be great to start, but you have to start to be great." - Zig Ziglar

"I experienced a major setback when I had a panic attack in public. But instead of giving up, I used it as an opportunity to learn and grow. I sought support, practiced self-care, and developed new coping strategies. Now, I'm more confident and resilient than ever." - Alex, age 29

Overcoming social anxiety is a journey, not a destination. Setbacks and relapses are temporary detours, but with the right mindset and strategies, you can stay on track and achieve your goals. Remember, progress is not linear, but it's worth it.

Tips for Staying on Track

1. Create a relapse prevention plan: Identify triggers and develop strategies to cope with them.
2. Practice self-care: Regularly engage in activities that bring you joy and relaxation.
3. Stay connected: Surround yourself with supportive people who encourage your progress.
4. Focus on progress, not perfection: Celebrate small victories and don't be too hard on yourself.

5. Be patient: Overcoming social anxiety takes time, effort, and perseverance.

"Success is not final, failure is not fatal: It is the courage to continue that counts." – Winston Churchill

Overcoming social anxiety is a journey that requires courage, resilience, and determination. By staying on track, overcoming setbacks, and focusing on progress, you can achieve your goals and live a more fulfilling life. Remember, you are not alone, and you are capable of overcoming any obstacle.

Remember, overcoming social anxiety is a process that takes time, effort, and patience. Stay committed, stay positive, and stay focused on your progress. You got this!

"You are stronger than you seem, braver than you believe, and smarter than you think." - Christopher Robin

Stay committed, stay flexible, and stay positive. You got this!

Chapter 14: Maintaining Momentum: Strategies for Long-Term Success

"Success is not a destination, it's a journey."

Overcoming social anxiety is a long-term process that requires maintaining momentum and consistency. It's easy to get started, but it's harder to stay on track. Here are some strategies to help you maintain momentum and achieve long-term success:

- Set Realistic Goals: Break down large goals into smaller, achievable ones.

"A journey of a thousand miles begins with a single step." – Lao Tzu

- Create a Support Network: Surround yourself with people who encourage and support you.

"Alone we can do so little; together we can do so much." – Helen Keller

- Practice Self-Care: Regularly engage in activities that bring you joy and relaxation.

"You can't pour from an empty cup. Take care of yourself first."

- Stay Positive: Focus on progress, not perfection.

"Believe you can and you're halfway there." - Theodore Roosevelt

- Embrace Challenges: View challenges as opportunities for growth and learning.

"The greatest glory in living lies not in never falling, but in rising every time we fall." – Nelson Mandela

- Stay Consistent: Make progress, not excuses.

"Consistency is key. Stay committed and stay focused."

- Celebrate Milestones: Acknowledge and celebrate your achievements.

"Celebrate your successes, no matter how small they may seem."

Maintaining momentum is crucial for overcoming social anxiety. By setting realistic goals, creating a support network, practicing self-care, staying positive, embracing challenges, staying consistent, and celebrating milestones, you can achieve long-term success. Remember, overcoming social anxiety is a journey, not a destination.

Additional Strategies for Maintaining Momentum

- Practice Mindfulness: Stay present and focused on the current moment.

"The present moment is the only moment available to us, and it is the door to all moments." – Thich Nhat Hanh

- Learn from Setbacks: Use setbacks as opportunities for growth and learning.

"Failure is not the opposite of success; it's part of success." – Arianna Huffington

- Stay Flexible: Be open to change and adjust your approach as needed.

"Be like a tree and let the dead leaves drop."

- Celebrate Small Wins: Acknowledge and celebrate small victories along the way.

"Small wins are a steady application of a small advantage." - Charles Duhigg

- Find Your Why: Connect with your purpose and reasons for overcoming social anxiety.

"Your why is the purpose, cause, or reason that drives

you and gives you direction." – Simon Sinek

Maintaining momentum is a crucial part of overcoming social anxiety. By incorporating these additional strategies into your daily life, you can stay on track and achieve long-term success. Remember, overcoming social anxiety is a journey, and it's okay to take it one step at a time.

Stay committed, stay focused, and stay positive. You got this!

"You are stronger than you seem, braver than you believe, and smarter than you think." - Christopher Robin

Chapter 15: Embracing Imperfection: Letting Go of Unrealistic Expectations

"Perfect is the enemy of good." – Voltaire

Social anxiety often stems from a desire to be perfect, to make a flawless impression, and to avoid judgment. However, this pursuit of perfection is not only unattainable but also detrimental to our mental health. Embracing imperfection is a crucial step in overcoming social anxiety.

The Problem with Perfectionism

"Perfectionism is a form of self-abuse."

Perfectionism sets unrealistically high standards, leading to self-criticism, anxiety, and burnout. It's essential to recognize that nobody is perfect, and it's okay to make mistakes.

"I'd rather be a failure at something I love than a success at something I hate." - George Burns

Embracing Imperfection

"Embracing imperfection is a sign of strength, not weakness."

Embracing imperfection involves:

- Accepting that mistakes are inevitable and valuable learning experiences
- Focusing on progress, not perfection
- Practicing self-compassion and self-forgiveness
- Letting go of unrealistic expectations and embracing authenticity

"You are imperfect, and you are wired for struggle, but you are worthy of love and belonging." - Brené Brown

Embracing imperfection is a liberating experience that allows us to let go of unrealistic expectations and focus on what truly matters. By accepting our imperfections, we can build resilience, develop self-compassion, and overcome social anxiety.

Remember, imperfection is a natural part of being

human. Embrace it, and you'll find freedom from the shackles of perfectionism.

"You are enough, just as you are."

The Power of Authenticity

"Authenticity is the daily practice of letting go of who we think we're supposed to be and embracing who we are." – Brené Brown

Embracing imperfection allows us to be authentic, to be ourselves without pretenses. Authenticity is the key to building meaningful relationships, finding self-acceptance, and overcoming social anxiety.

"The most courageous act is still to think for yourself. Aloud." - Coco Chanel

Letting Go of Unrealistic Expectations

"You can't start the next chapter of your life if you keep re-reading the last one." - Unknown

Letting go of unrealistic expectations means:

- Accepting that we can't control everything
- Embracing uncertainty and ambiguity
- Focusing on what we can control, our actions and reactions
- Practicing self-compassion and self-forgiveness

"You are not a mistake. You are not a problem to be solved. You are a unique and valuable person."

"Embracing imperfection and letting go of unrealistic expectations is a powerful step in overcoming social anxiety. By being authentic, accepting ourselves, and focusing on what truly matters, we can build resilience, develop self-compassion, and live a more fulfilling life."

Remember, you are enough, just as you are. Embrace your imperfections, and you'll find freedom from the shackles of perfectionism.

Popular Quote: "Love yourself first, and everything else falls into line." - Lucille Ball

Conclusion

Chapter 16: The Journey Ahead: Embracing a Life of Confidence and Connection

"The future belongs to those who believe in the beauty of their dreams." – Eleanor Roosevelt

Overcoming social anxiety is a journey, not a destination. It takes time, effort, and patience, but the reward is a life of confidence, connection, and purpose.

Embracing a Life of Confidence

"Confidence is not 'they will like me'. Confidence is 'I'll be fine if they don't'."

Confidence is not the absence of fear, but the willingness to take action despite fear. It's built through small victories, self-compassion, and a growth mindset.

"You don't have to be great to start, but you have to

start to be great." – Zig Ziglar

Cultivating Connection

"The best way to find yourself is to lose yourself in the service of others." – Mahatma Gandhi

Connection is the foundation of a fulfilling life. It's built through empathy, active listening, and vulnerability.

"Alone we can do so little; together we can do so much." – Helen Keller

The Power of Vulnerability

"Vulnerability is the birthplace of love, belonging, and creativity."
– Brené Brown

Vulnerability is the key to deep connections and meaningful relationships. It takes courage, but it's worth it.

"You are never too old to set another goal or to dream a new dream." - C.S. Lewis

The Journey Ahead

"Life is 10% what happens to you and 90% how you react to it." - Charles R. Swindoll

The journey ahead won't be easy, but it will be worth it. Remember to be patient, kind, and compassionate with yourself.

"You are stronger than you seem, braver than you believe, and smarter than you think." – Christopher Robin

Overcoming social anxiety is a journey that requires courage, resilience, and determination. But the reward is a life of confidence, connection, and purpose. Embrace the journey ahead, and remember that you are capable of achieving greatness.

Remember, the future belongs to those who believe in the beauty of their dreams. Believe in yourself, and you'll be unstoppable.

Embracing the Unknown

"The unknown is not something to be feared, but something to be explored."

The journey ahead is full of unknowns, but that's what makes it exciting. Embrace the unknown, and you'll discover new opportunities and experiences.

"The biggest risk is not taking any risk." - Mark Zuckerberg

Staying Positive and Focused

"Keep your eyes on the stars, and your feet on the ground." - Theodore Roosevelt

Stay positive and focused on your goals, even when faced with challenges and setbacks. Remember why you started, and let that motivate you to keep moving forward.

"Fall seven times, stand up eight." – Japanese proverb

Surrounding Yourself with Support

"Surround yourself with people who believe in you."

Surround yourself with people who support and encourage you. Having a positive network will help you stay motivated and inspired.

"The people you surround yourself with are the people you become."

The journey ahead is full of possibilities and opportunities. Embrace the unknown, stay positive and focused, and surround yourself with support. Remember, overcoming social anxiety is a journey, not a destination. Enjoy the process, and celebrate your successes along the way.

Remember, you got this! You are capable of achieving greatness and living a life of confidence and connection. Keep moving forward, and never give up on your dreams.

www.ingramcontent.com/pod-product-compliance
Lightning Source LLC
Chambersburg PA
CBHW070832250726

48662CB00003B/1185